Zoom fun™

outside

Compiled by Amy E. Sklansky

Little, Brown and Company

Boston   New York   London

First Edition

ZOOM, ZOOMer, ZOOMguest, ZOOMsci, ZOOMchat, ZOOMgames, ZOOMzone, ZOOMjournal, ZOOMdo, ZOOMparty, Zoops, Zoinks!, whatZup, CafeZOOM, ZOOMzingers, ZOOMfun, ZOOMerang, ZOOMa Cum Laude, ZOOMmedia, Ubbi Dubbi, Zfact, Zmail, ZOOMkids, By Kids, for Kids, Fannee Doolee, and other composite ZOOM marks contained herein are trademarks of the WGBH Educational Foundation. Zoinks!™ compiled by Bill Shribman.

Library of Congress Cataloging-in-Publication Data
ZOOMfun outside / compiled by Amy E. Sklansky. — 1st ed.
       p. cm.
       Summary: Presents more than fifty outdoor activities, games, experiments and some fun features from the popular television show, ZOOM.
       ISBN 0-316-95278-8
       1. Outdoor recreation for children—Juvenile literature. 2. ZOOM (Television program : WGBH (Television station : Boston, Mass.))—Juvenile literature. [1. Outdoor recreation. 2. Amusements.] I. Sklansky, Amy E.

GV182.9 .Z66 2000
796—dc21   99-047324

10 9 8 7 6 5 4 3 2 1

Q-KPT

Printed in the United States of America

"Capture a Spiderweb" activity adapted from the ZOOMkit™ Spider Frame. Ivory Snow is a registered trademark owned by the Proctor & Gamble Company. Popsicle is a registered trademark owned by Popsicle Industries, Inc. Spam is a registered trademark owned by the Hormel Foods Corporation. All brand-name products are trademarks of their respective owners.

Funding for ZOOM is provided by public television viewers, the National Science Foundation, and the Corporation for Public Broadcasting.

Design by WGBH Design

Photo credits: copyright page: Mark Ostow; pages 2–3: Mark Ostow; page 6: Mark Ostow; page 18: Lisa Abitbol; page 19: Mark Ostow; page 39: Lisa Abitbol; page 51: Lisa Abitbol, Mark Ostow; page 52: Mark Ostow; page 56: Lisa Abitbol; page 57: Lisa Abitbol, Mark Ostow; page 58: Lisa Abitbol; page 59: Mark Ostow; page 60: Mark Ostow, Bill Shribman; page 61: Bill Shribman, Steve Offsey.

Illustration credits: pages 8–9: Amity Femia; page 10: Steve Schudlich; page 13: Amity Femia; pages 14–15: Amity Femia; page 16: Steve Schudlich; page 20: Amity Femia; pages 22–23: Steve Schudlich; pages 26–27: Amity Femia; page 28: Steve Schudlich; page 30: Amity Femia; page 50: Amity Femia; page 56: Amity Femia.

Hey ZOOMers,

ZOOM is TV by kids, for kids. **Without you,** there wouldn't be a show! Everything you see on ZOOM was sent in by kids from all over the country.

Each show is a **cool mix** of games, experiments, crafts, kid guests, recipes, brainteasers, jokes, skits, and more. After watching, you'll want to try them all yourself.

But ZOOM is more than TV. We have a Web site at **pbskids.org/zoom** and our own newsletter called ZOOMerang. So check us out when you're surfing the Internet. Send us your ideas by mail or e-mail, and we'll send you the latest edition of ZOOMerang and consider putting your ideas on the show or our site.

All ZOOM segments, except ZOOMguest and whatZup, are taped inside the TV studio. But lots of the things we do on ZOOM are even *more fun* when you do them outside. In this book you'll find our top picks for **ZOOMfun outside.** You'll discover new ways to explore, play, and even eat outdoors. So grab this book, head outside, and don't forget to close the door behind you.

What are you waiting for?
C'mon and ZOOM outside!

Jessica
Claudio
Ray!
Caroline
Alisa
Zoe
Kenny

P.S. *Check out* the last page to find out how to send your ideas to ZOOM.

Explore Outside

Play Outside

Huburruby ubup! Gubet rubeadubing uband hubead uboutsubide!

What? You can't understand what she's saying? That's because she's speaking Ubbi Dubbi, ZOOM's secret language. We promise to reveal the secret to speaking Ubbi Dubbi before this book ends—so keep reading!

Eat Outside

whatZup!

Everything You Always Wanted to Know about ZOOM

Meet Stephen
King of the Castles

Q: How old are you and where do you live?

Stephen: I'm twelve years old and I live near the Pacific coast, one of the largest sand-castle construction sites in the world!

Q: What are your secrets for building great sand castles?

Stephen: There are two techniques for building a sand castle: form technique and volcano technique.

Q: Can you explain form technique?

Stephen: With form technique you take any kind of container and pack it *tight* with wet sand. You turn it upside down, lift off the mold, and that is the beginning of your castle. You can use any kind of container, like a flowerpot, a cake mold, or a bucket. This technique is good for buildings, houses, and castles.

Q: Can you explain volcano technique?

Stephen: The idea of volcano technique is pushing a lot of sand into a pile that looks a little like a volcano. Then you can pour water on the sand to make it stronger. Keep doing this until you've made your volcano the size you want. You can shape it any way you like. This technique is good for making animals, people, and plants.

Q: Any other tips for sand-castle builders?

Stephen: No matter what technique you use, once you've got the basic structure, you can fill in the details by sculpting or adding shells, stones, or seaweed.

The Lost City of Atlantis—form technique.

Permanent Sand Castle

Sent in by Stephanie N. of Sharon, Massachusetts.

If you're not near a beach, you can still build a sand castle—and this one won't get washed away by the tide!

You will need:

- 2 cups sawdust (You can usually get it free at a hardware store or lumberyard.)
- 1 cup wallpaper-paste powder (You can buy this at a hardware store.)
- 1 cup water
- cans, paper cups, and empty milk cartons to use as molds
- utensils or toothpicks for sculpting and molding

optional: glue, seashells, paper flags, tiny paper umbrellas

Mix the sawdust and wallpaper-paste powder with your hands in a large bowl. Add the water and continue until well mixed.

Pack the mixture into your mold. **Flip** the mold upside down and carefully remove it. **Patch** the castle if necessary. Sculpt details and designs with utensils or toothpicks.

Let the castle **dry** in a sunny place for a few days.

P.S. If you want to decorate, wait until the castle is dry. Then glue on seashells, flags, or umbrellas. You can also make more castles to create your own sand city.

Ice Castle

If it's wintertime and you feel like building a castle, why not make an ice castle?

You will need:

- a variety of plastic containers
- water
- spray bottle filled with water
- plastic or rubber gloves
- food coloring (optional)

Note: Rubber gloves should be worn to protect your skin when handling ice shapes. Otherwise, the ice might stick to your skin.

Fill a number of containers with water and put them outside to freeze overnight. Or, if you live in a place where the weather is warm, put them in your freezer instead. If you would like parts of your castle to be colored, **add** food coloring to the water first. When the water is frozen, **dip** the containers in warm water so the shapes will come out more easily. Place the shapes any way you like. When stacking ice shapes on top of each other, spray the top of the bottom shape with water. Then **hold** the two shapes in place for a few seconds until they are frozen together.

P.S. If you make your ice castle in the freezer, you can enjoy it by placing it in a punch bowl filled with punch. It will look great *and* keep things cool.

Fannee Doolee

likes **blizzards** but doesn't like **snow.** Why do you think that is?

My family has a tradition that every year on the first snowstorm we build a gigantic snowhouse with underground tunnels, windows — the works.

Snow Art

Ever get tired of that same old white snow in your yard? Try this!

You will need:

containers, such as sprayers, basters, or water guns
water
food coloring

Fill the containers with colored water and take them outside to paint a masterpiece on your snow canvas (your snow-covered lawn or sidewalk).

Zfact:

In **I cup** of snow, there are **10 million** snowflakes.

Zfact:

The **largest** snowflake ever measured was **15 inches** across.

Ask an adult to help you use the electric mixer.

Unmeltable Snowman

If it's not snowing where you live, but you feel like making a snowman anyway, try this.

You will need:

- 2 cups soap flakes, such as Ivory Snow
- $1/2$ cup water
- several toothpicks
- electric mixer
- decorations, such as beads, twigs, candies, and yarn

Pour soap flakes and water into a bowl. **Whip** with an electric mixer until the mixture is doughy. Use your hands to **mold** the mixture into 3 balls. **Attach** the balls together with toothpicks. **Decorate** your snowman any way you like. It will take a few hours for the snowman to dry. As it dries, it will become whiter.

Stargazing

Next time you're outside on a clear night, **look overhead** at the stars. (They're also in the sky in the daytime, but it's too light to see them.) A star is **a ball of hot, glowing gases.** The nearest star to Earth is the Sun. The Sun is **93 million miles away** from Earth, which is pretty close compared to the next nearest star, which is more than 24 *trillion* miles away!

The stars you see in the sky depend upon **where you live and what time of year** it is. From Earth it seems that the position of the stars is always changing. This is because Earth is **constantly spinning, and revolving** around the Sun. A group of stars, called a constellation, that you see in winter may look upside down when you see it in summer. Below are tips for identifying constellations such as Orion, the Big Dipper, and the Little Dipper. If you want to learn about other stars, head for your local library or surf the Internet.

The constellation **Orion** is named after a Greek hero who was a great hunter. It is best seen from December to April. **Look for his belt first**—it is made up of three stars. Betelgeuse is part of Orion and is the largest star that can be seen with the naked eye. It is **700 times** the size of the Sun, but looks smaller because it is so far away.

Orion in November

Orion in January

Orion in April

Orion

Zfact:

Our galaxy, the Milky Way, contains about **100,000 million** stars. About every **18 days** our galaxy gives birth to a new star.

Big Dipper and Little Dipper in Spring

Big Dipper and Little Dipper in Winter

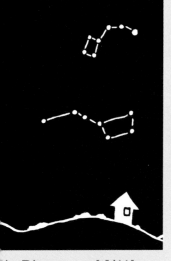

Big Dipper and Little Dipper in Autumn

Big Dipper and Little Dipper in Summer

Zfact:

A shooting star isn't actually a star at all. It is a **meteor,** a piece of space rock, burning up as it travels through Earth's atmosphere. Watch the sky August through December and you're likely to see some.

The Big Dipper is **made up of seven stars** and is one of the easier constellations to spot in the Northern Hemisphere. The Little Dipper is also made up of seven stars and can always **be found near** the Big Dipper.

If you extend an imaginary line from the bottom of the bowl of the Big Dipper, you will find the North Star. The North Star, also called Polaris, is always found in the same place in the sky. Other stars, like those in the Big Dipper and Little Dipper, appear to circle around it. Sailors used to navigate by Polaris because it hovers above the North Pole.

Note: Orion and the Big Dipper and Little Dipper can only be seen in the Northern Hemisphere.

9

Recycled Bird Feeder

E-mailed by Samantha D.

Birds live everywhere. You will find them living near you whether you live in the country or the city. You can get to know the birds in your neighborhood by building a bird feeder. Here's how:

First, **punch** a hole in the top of the milk carton and put a string through the hole. Carefully **cut** the milk carton starting 5½ inches up from the bottom. **Start** in the middle of one side and cut all the way around to the middle of the opposite side. Then go back to where you started and cut down about 3 inches, then back around to the opposite side, and then cut up until you meet the other cut. This will be a doorway.

You will need:

- clean, dry half-gallon milk carton
- ruler
- scissors
- string
- birdseed

Next, **fill** the carton with birdseed until it reaches the hole you cut in the side. Using the string, **hang** the carton on a tree branch or something else outside.

Check your feeder in the morning and in the evening. Keep track of how many birds you see. Do you see more birds in the morning or in the evening? Do you know what kinds they are?

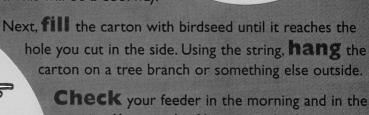

"The birds love my feeder. Our main bird feeder is out in the open. Mine hangs under a tree branch, which gives the birds a little more protection. I get lots of birds each day with sunflower seeds. I see mostly chickadees and tufted titmice."
— e-mail from Tori M. of Dover, Massachusetts

Pinecone Bird Feeder

Sent in by Caurie D. of Carrollton, Georgia.

If you want to make an all-natural bird feeder, try this one.

You will need:
- medium-sized pinecone
- peanut butter
- spoon
- birdseed
- string

Tie about 2 feet of string around the top section of the pinecone. With a spoon, **smear** peanut butter all over the pinecone. Then **roll** the pinecone in a bowl of birdseed until it is completely covered.

Tie the string to a tree and watch the birds come!

Hint: You can feed birds after a snowfall by sprinkling birdseed in your snowy yard or park in a fun shape, like a heart, a smiley face, or even your name.

Kristen and Devon of Groton, Massachusetts, like to bird-watch in their backyard.

For a closer look at birds, check out these guides and Web sites:

- *Backyard Birds (Peterson Field Guides for Young Naturalists)*, Houghton Mifflin.
- *National Audubon Society's First Field Guides: Birds*, Scholastic.
- *Birds of the World (Eyewitness Handbooks)* by Alan Greensmith; Dorling Kindersley.
- *Birding* by Joseph Forshaw, Steve Howell, Terence Lindsey, and Rich Stallcup; Time-Life Books.
- http://birdsource.cornell.edu
- http://birdwatching.com
- http://audubon.org

Meet Rebecca
and Some Wiggly Worms

Q: How old are you and where do you live?
Rebecca: I'm ten years old and I live in Memphis, Tennessee.

Q: How do you find worms?
Rebecca: A good time to find them is early morning or evening. Look under a rock or a log because it's dark and moist under there and that's where they like to hide. The reason I feel around in the dirt instead of just looking is because I really can't see. I was born blind. I have to use my sense of touch to find out where they are. Worms can't see or hear so they have to use their sense of touch to know that I'm there, and then they'll try to get away from me.

Q: Can you tell us some interesting facts about worms?
Rebecca: I know that earthworms are called annelids. Annelids are segmented worms. Their bodies are divided into many little rings or segments. These segments help the worm move through the dirt, sort of like a Slinky. The segments expand and the head moves forward. Then the body contracts and pulls itself closer to the head. Also, on the segments of the worm are tiny hairs called setae. Setae help grip the dirt as the worm moves. You can't feel or see the setae because they're so small, but I know about them because I read about them in a braille book. I guess that makes me a book-worm!

Q: What's your favorite thing about studying worms?
Rebecca: Being outside. I was made for the out-doors!

Build a Worm Farm

Make a worm farm and get a close-up view of **worms at work.** Worms eat their way through soil. They digest the soil and it passes out of their bodies as waste called *castings*. The castings make the soil better for growing. The tunnels left by the worms also help things grow because they make the soil airier.

You will need:

- large glass jar with lid
- sand
- dark garden soil
- worms
- rotting leaves or other compost (see Compost Column on p. 28)
- spray bottle filled with water
- sheet of black paper
- tape
- scissors

leaves

soil

sand

Ask an adult to help you **poke** a few holes in the lid. **Pour** about 1½ inches of sand into the bottom of the jar. **Smooth** out the surface of the sand. Repeat with a layer of soil. Alternate layers a few more times, ending with a layer of soil. **Add** 3 or 4 worms to the top layer of soil. Put rotten leaves or compost on top, then lightly **spray** with water. **Wrap** the black paper around the outside of the jar to keep things nice and dark for the worms. Screw on the lid.

After a couple of days, **remove** the paper and observe the worms' work. You should see tunnels and a shifting of the layers of soil and sand. Spray with water every few days to keep the soil **moist,** but not wet. (Worms breathe through their skin. If the soil is really wet, they will drown or be forced to the surface.)

Here's a joke from Frankie R. of Mesquite, New Mexico:

Why didn't Noah go fishing in his ark?

Answer: He only had two worms.

Go Fly a Kite!

Zfact:

People have been flying kites since ancient Egypt. Kites have a history of being **tools** as well as **toys**. They have been used to test atmospheric electricity, temperature, wind velocity, barometric pressure, and humidity. They were even used for target practice by soldiers during World War II.

Of course, you'll need a kite before you can fly one. Here's how to make one yourself! This kite is called a Scott sled kite and was invented in the 1950s.

You will need:

- permanent marker
- ruler
- rectangular piece of a plastic garbage bag (39 x 35 inches)
- scissors
- 2 wooden dowels or sticks (35 inches)
- tape
- large craft needle
- kite string

1 **Measure,** trace, and cut the plastic to match the dimensions shown in the diagram.

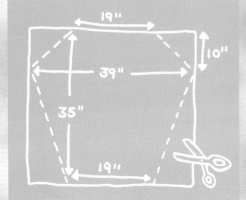

2 Then **cut** a triangular hole near the bottom of the kite as shown.

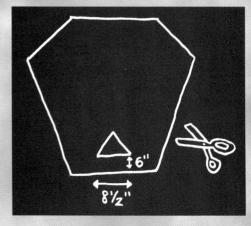

14

3 **Tape** the dowels to the kite as shown. Then stick a 1-inch piece of tape to both corners to strengthen the area where the bridle string will be attached. (See next step.)

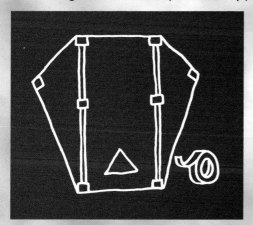

4 **Measure** and cut a 5-foot piece of string to be the bridle string. With your needle, make a hole in both reinforced corners and thread the string through the holes. **Tie** a knot in each end of the string. Note: Make sure you measure the string accurately — this can affect the launching of your kite.

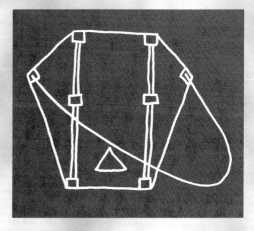

P.S. You might try adding streamers or ribbons to the back end of your kite. Experiment to see which lengths work. If they are too long or heavy, the kite will not fly. If you want to decorate your kite, try fabric paint or paint pens that are made to work on plastic.

Warning: Never fly a kite near power lines or during high winds or thunderstorms!

5 **Find** the center of your bridle string. Tie your flying line to that spot.

The next time it's windy outside, find an open space where you can **run** fast and where your kite won't get caught in a tree. Beaches and ball fields are good bets. Launching a kite is usually the most difficult part of kite flying. Try to let your kite out slowly until it catches the wind.

Can You Hear the Temperature

Sent in by Megann H. of North Little Rock, Arkansas.

Want to know how hot it is outside but don't have a thermometer? A **cricket** can tell you if you **listen** closely.

Most crickets chirp faster when it's hot outside To find out the temperature (in degrees Fahrenheit), **count** the number of chirps you hear in 13 seconds, then **add** 40 to that number.

Use a regular thermometer to **test** your results. How close were you? T number may not be exact because crickets chirp differently when they feel threatened. But this fo mula should get you pretty close to the actual tempe ature. Try it and see i it works!

The Slug's Thanksgiving Song
A Poem

For leaves and greens and nice damp places.
For flowers and roots and deep dark spaces.
For sticky slime that helps me go,
even though I am quite slow.
For hardened skin that helps me hide
from birds and beasts and things outside.
For all this I'm thankful.

Sent in by Leanna B. of Belmont, Massachusetts.

Capture a Spiderweb

You will need:

- 1 spiderweb
- hair spray
- baby powder
- black construction paper
- scissors

First be sure the spider is not in the web! **Spray** the web with hair spray to make it sticky. **Sprinkle** the web with a light dusting of powder. **Spray** the black paper with hair spray. **Press** the hair spray side of the paper against the web. **Hold** the paper steady while your helper cuts the web loose from its supports.

Most spiders don't harm people, but there are a few poisonous kinds. Please ask an adult before handling any spider.

Want to learn more about spiders? Look for books like these:

National Audubon Society Pocket Guide: Insects and Spiders, by John Farrand Jr.; Knopf.

Spiders, by Gail Gibbons; Holiday House.

Spiders, by Jenny Tesar; Blackbirch Press.

Web Weavers and Other Spiders, by Bobbie Kalman; Crabtree Publishing Company.

zfacts:

A spider has no **nose** or **tongue.** Scientists believe that a spider tastes and smells with its **feet!** Spiders **eat** by injecting their victims with a special liquid that breaks down the insect's insides into a liquid that can be sucked out and consumed by the spider.

A spider doesn't **stick** to its web because its body is covered with special **oil.** Also, only **some** of the threads are sticky—the spider knows which to avoid.

Bubble-Blowing Bonanza

To make a blower, put a piece of string through two straws and tie it at the ends. Then arrange the straws on the string as in the diagram. You can make a larger version of this blower using tubing and clothesline. To make a different kind of blower, bend and twist the coat hanger into a rounded shape with a handle. *Ask an adult to help you because edges can be sharp.*

Mix water, dishwashing liquid, and glycerin. **Dip** a blower the mixture. Slowly **lift** it out and hold it up to the wind You may need to blow on it or move it slowly to get t bubbles started. See who can blow the biggest bub

You will need:

- string
- straws
- clear plastic tubing
- clothesline
- wire coat hanger
- 1 cup dishwashing liquid
- 12 cups water
- 3–4 tablespoons glycerin (from the drugstore)
- large baking pan or laundry tub

What's your favorite thing to do outside?

"Jump ramps with my skates on."
—Neal H. of Augusta, Georgia

"To sit and watch the clouds and just relax!" —Kenny

"Lie on a raft in the lake with my mom." —Jessica J. of East Rochester, New York

"I like going out when new seasons are beginning—the colors of fall and that smell when winter's starting." —Alisa

"Dance in the rain."
—Akash G. of Martinez, Georgia

"I like taking walks with my mom and I LOVE going camping with my family!" —Jessica

How about you?

19

Make a Mushroom Print

You will need:

- 1 mushroom (any kind with visible gills)
- knife
- paper
- glass bowl or jar
- hair spray

Ask an adult to **cut** the stem off your mushroom and, if necessary, trim around the lower edges of the cap so that the gills are exposed. **Place** the mushroom on the paper with the gills facing down. A mushroom's gills contain millions of tiny spores that may someday grow into new mushrooms. **Put** the glass container over the mushroom and let it sit overnight. The glass prevents the spores from blowing away. The next day, **lift** off the glass and lift up your mushroom. You should see a lovely spore print.

Warning: Never eat a mushroom you find outside. Many kinds are poisonous!

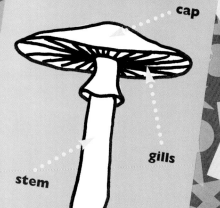

cap

gills

stem

Raindrop Painting

Next time it rains, don't get sad — get creative! Who needs a paintbrush when you have raindrops?

You will need:
uncoated white paper plate
food coloring
white crayon

Use the white crayon to **draw** a pattern or any picture you like on the paper plate. Then **sprinkle** a few drops of food coloring onto the plate. Throw on your raincoat and head outside with the plate. Set it down and watch as the raindrops cause the colors to run and splatter. The area colored with crayon will **resist** the colors. When you think it looks finished, take it back inside to dry.

Here's a **joke** from Bobby M. of Apple Creek, Ohio:

What did Mrs. Claus say to Santa during the thunderstorm?

Answer: Watch out for that rain, dear.

Zfacts:

As soon as you see lightning, start counting the seconds until you hear thunder. If **5 seconds** pass, the storm is **1 mile** away. A **10-second** delay means it is **2 miles** away, etc. If you see lightning flash but don't hear any thunder, then the storm may be as far away as **15 miles.**

Have the **rain** clouds got you down? Why not use some fabric paint to create a **cheery** design on an old umbrella? But wait a day for the paint to dry before using your umbrella, or the rain will wash away all your hard work!

21

Fantastic

Sent in by Meghan S. and Lee M. of College Station, Arkansas.

1

This activity can get **messy,** which is why it's great to do outside. If you have to do it inside, **cover** the launch area with newspaper.

To make the rocket body, **roll** a piece of construction paper once around the film canister to form a long tube. **Tape** the paper to the canister. The paper should not **extend** past the rim of the open end of the canister.

Ask an adult to help you with this experiment.

"My rocket went ten feet. I showed it to my class. They really loved it."
—e-mail from Andrew A. of Danville, Pennsylvania

"I found out that you can also do this with an Alka-Seltzer tablet and water!"
—e-mail from Hans V. of Avon Park, Florida

2

Make a **nose** cone by cutting a circle out of construction paper. It should be bigger than the opening of the tube. Cut a **straight** line from the edge of the circle to the center point. **Slide** the cut edges past each other to form a cone. **Tape** it together. Then tape the cone to the top of the rocket body—the end opposite the canister.

Film-Canister

Rocket

3 **Fuel** the rocket by putting the baking soda onto two sheets of toilet paper. **Fold** the paper around the baking soda to make a packet. (This will delay the chemical reaction.) **Put** the fuel packet in the film canister.

Pour vinegar into the film canister and quickly put on the lid. **Set** the rocket down on a flat surface with the nose cone pointing up. Quickly **move** away from the launch site and wait for blastoff! **(Note: This is not dangerous.)**

How **high** did your rocket launch?

P.S. Experiment with different amounts of baking soda and vinegar to get your rocket to fly its highest. What happens when you change the shape of the nose cone?

Why do baking soda and vinegar make good fuel for your rocket?

When you **combine** baking soda and vinegar inside the canister, a chemical reaction occurs. The mixture **creates** a gas called carbon dioxide. As more gas is created by the reaction, the pressure **builds** up until there is enough gas to push off the top of the canister.

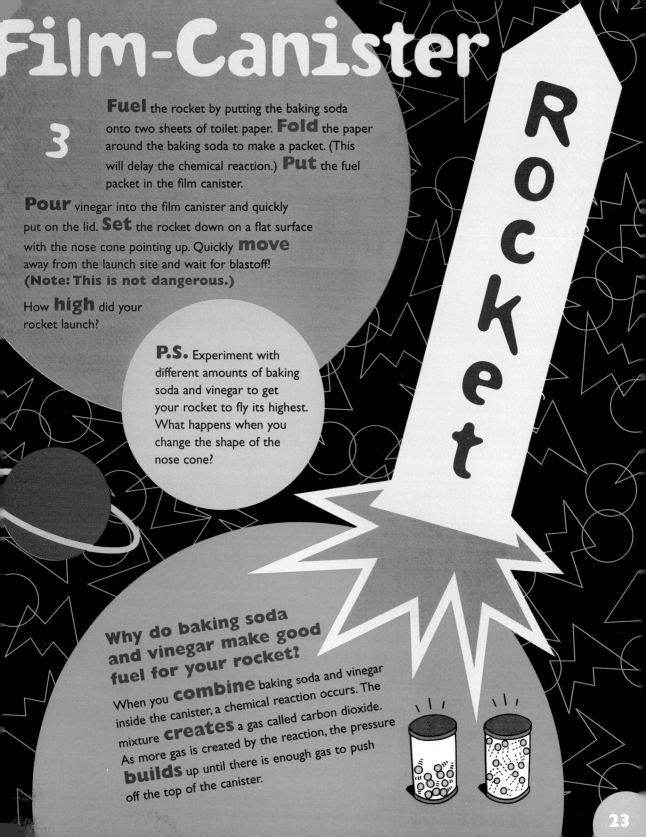

Super Soda-Bottle Boat

Get busy with the fizzy and make your own speedboat!

Sent in by Steven B. of Fayetteville, Arkansas.

You will need:

- **2-liter plastic soda bottle**
- **thumbtack**
- **toilet paper**
- **baking soda**
- **vinegar**
- **marbles or pebbles**

Zoop

"The funniest thing that ever happened to me was when I was sitting by my pool and a bird pooped on my head."
— Kelsey L. of Rocky River, Ohio

"To make it go faster, I left the cap on loosely, and I made a hole in the cap."
—e-mail from Allison of New Hyde Park, New York

"My brother and I each built our own soda-bottle boat! Then we had a race. Guess who won? Not me! My brother Holden won."
—e-mail from Gaven C. of Esko, Minnesota

Using the thumbtack, make a hole in the **cap** of the soda bottle. Lay down 3 or 4 sheets of **toilet paper** and put some baking soda on them. Spread the baking soda out evenly and **roll up** the toilet paper. (The paper slows down the reaction between the baking soda and the vinegar.)

Put the rolled-up toilet paper into the soda bottle. Add some marbles or pebbles to the cap end of the bottle so that it is **weighted** down and the cap is in the water. **Fill** the bottle a quarter of the way with vinegar and quickly put the cap on the bottle.

Place your boat in a full **tub** or plastic **pool** and watch it go! (Note: This is not dangerous.)

You can also make the boat without poking a hole — just **loosen** the cap.

P.S. Can you make your boat travel **faster?** What could you change about your design? What would happen if you changed the **amounts** of baking soda and vinegar? What about changing the **temperature** of the vinegar?

Lovely Leaf Rubbings

You will need:

- several different kinds of leaves
- thin white paper
- dark-colored crayons

When leaves change color in the fall, **collect** several that are not dry or crumbly. Arrange up to 4 leaves on a smooth surface. **Lay** a thin sheet of white paper over the leaves. Remove the wrapping from around a dark-colored crayon. Using the side of the crayon, **rub** gently over your paper. Watch as the outlines and vein lines of your leaves appear on the paper.

You can **use** your leaf rubbing as stationery or plain old decoration.

Fannee Doolee likes **yellow** and **green,** but doesn't like **violet** and **red.** Why do you think that is?

26

Look Through a Leaf Window

You will need:

- newspaper
- waxed paper
- several leaves
- an iron
- scissors
- small crayon pieces (optional)

Ask an adult to help you **heat** the iron on low (or on the wool setting). Place a piece of newspaper on your ironing board or table. Then lay a piece of waxed paper on top of it and arrange the leaves. If you like, **sprinkle** some small crayon pieces around the leaves. Lay a sheet of waxed paper on top of the leaves and lay a piece of newspaper over that. With an adult's help, **iron** the newspaper to seal the waxed paper and press your leaves. Use your scissors to even out the edges of your "window" or to cut out different shapes.

Hint: You might want to cut out a section of your leaf window to make an ornament. Just punch a hole in it and tie on a piece of string.

Zoinks!

Many of the ZOOM staffers have pets. What kind? Here's a list: dogs, cats, hermit crabs, a frog, guinea pigs, a raven, a hamster, gerbils, and an iguana.

What did they name their pets? Sebastian, Terwilligger, Leo, Lope, Dancia, Stubb, Hukwa, Mouse (This one is actually a cat!), Daisy, Per, Gawain, Uther, Ira, Lulu, Cinderella, Lucy, and Farfel.

Which name do you think goes best with each pet?

P.S. If you want to **find** out when the leaves are changing **color** near where you live, call the Fall Foliage Hotline sponsored by the U.S. Forest Service at **1-800-354-4595.**

Create a COMPOST Column

Sent in by Taylor T. of Longview, Texas.

Learn how to make compost and **recycle** kitchen garbage into dark, rich soil. You can add the compost to houseplants, use some in a worm farm (see p. 13), or add it to your garden as a fertilizer. But the best thing about compost is that you are **reducing** the amount of trash you and your family produce.

You will need:

- scissors
- 3 two-liter soda bottles with labels removed
- 2 bottle caps
- thumbtack
- masking or packing tape
- vegetable and fruit scraps or yard waste (grass clippings, dead leaves, etc.)
- soil

Zfact:

Each person in the United States throws out about 4 pounds of garbage every day.

Cut bottles as shown. Use the thumbtack to **poke** holes in one bottle cap. Then **screw** it onto Bottle B.

Ask an adult to help you cut the bottle. Edges can be sharp.

A (lid)

Insert Bottle B upside down into Bottle C. **Tape** Bottles B and C together. Insert Bottle A into the open end of Bottle B and tape them together.

Add the scraps and yard waste. (Do NOT add meat or dairy scraps or your compost will be really smelly!!) **Moisten** the materials well with water. Place the top section of Bottle A on top of the rest of Bottle A and tape them together. Carefully **shake** the column to mix the water and compost ingredients. Any extra water will drain to the bottom section.

Check your Compost Column daily. If it appears to be drying out, you can add a little more water, but don't add any if there's still some in the bottom section.

"When I tried the compost project, it really worked!!! I used it in our garden and now our crops are growing over my head!!"
—Breanna C. of Esko, Minnesota

Grow Sunflowers and Bake Salty Sunflower Seeds

Do you have a green thumb? Find out by planting some sunflower seeds.

You will need:

sunflower seeds (You can buy these at a nursery.)
an area of soil for planting, or a 4-gallon container and potting soil and sand
water

Choose a **sunny** spot. Plant seeds about 2 feet apart and ³/₄ inch deep. If you're using a container, mix equal parts potting soil and sand and fill the container. **Water** the seeds when the soil is dry. You should see sprouts in about a week. Once flowers start forming, water the plants a little more often.

You can **harvest** your sunflower seeds when the backs of the flowers turn yellow. Cut the stems about 1 or 2 feet below the flowers. **Hang** them upside down to dry completely in a cool, dark place. This will take about 3 to 4 weeks.

When the flowers are dry, **pick** out the seeds. You can put some in your bird feeder. **Soak** the rest in saltwater overnight. Drain and spread them on a cookie sheet. Ask an adult to help you **bake** them at 200 degrees until they're crisp (about 1¹/₂ hours). Enjoy!

Fannee Doolee

loves **trees** but hates the **forest.** Why do you think that is?

Before you go hiking or camping, you might want to **surf** the Web and check out these sites:

National Park Service at **http://www.nps.gov/**

Great Outdoor Recreation Pages at **http://www.gorp.com**

Appalachian Mountain Club at **http://www.outdoors.or**

Trailplace, an interactive Web site for Appalachian Trail thru-hikers at **http://www.trailplace.com**

Camping-USA! at **http://www.camping-usa.com**

On a Hike

Wherever you live, there are places to hike: in the mountains, in the desert, near a lake or river, or in a city park. **Remember** to bring these things with you on your next hike:

- an adult who knows the woods
- sturdy, broken-in shoes
- watch
- map
- matches
- sunblock
- small flashlight
- layers of clothing (You may get hotter or colder as you hike.)
- food (Light, dry foods are best.)
- water (DON'T forget this one!)

Next time you go for a hike, keep an **eye** out for trail signs. And maybe you'd like to **leave** trail messages for someone else. Here's what you **need** to know:

Rock Signs

This is the trail.

Turn left.

Turn right.

Important warning:

Grass Signs

This is the trail.

Turn left.

Turn right.

Important warning:

Happy hiking!

Reading Animal Tracks

No matter where you live, you can always find animal tracks nearby. You can find them in the park, on a beach, or in your backyard. Tracks are especially easy to see when the ground is muddy or snowy.

Can you **guess** who made these tracks?

Next time you're outside, see if you can find some tracks to read.

1. seagull 2. cat 3. deer 4. dog 5. frog 6. raccoon 7. human 8. rabbit

S'mores and More

Besides sleeping outside, one of the best parts of a campout is the campfire. Swap ghost stories while you make this classic campfire snack:

You will need:
- large marshmallows
- stick or hanger for roasting
- plain chocolate bar
- graham crackers

If you're in the mood for camping out, but are stuck **inside** with a microwave instead of a campfire, try this:

Ask an adult to help you whenever you use a microwave.

Put half a graham cracker on a paper plate and put some chocolate on top. **Heat** in the microwave for about 15 seconds. Remove from the microwave. Put the other half of the graham cracker on a different plate and put a marshmallow on top. Heat in the microwave for about 15 seconds. Then **smoosh** the two halves together to form a sandwich. Let cool for about a minute and eat.

Sent in by Olivia H. of New York City, New York.

An adult should always be present around a campfire. Campfires should be lit in a fire pit surrounded by rocks or in a special hole dug in the ground. Water and a shovel should be nearby for putting out the fire.

Break a graham cracker in half. **Put** some chocolate on one half of the cracker and set the other half aside.

When the fire dies down a bit, **roast** a marshmallow over the red-hot coals. Don't rush things—a perfectly roasted marshmallow takes time, but is worth it! When your marshmallow is a golden brown color, carefully pull it off your roasting stick and place it on top of the chocolate. (The marshmallow will be hot!) Use the second half of the graham cracker to form the lid to your s'more sandwich.

Mmmm... Anybody want s'more?

Fascinating Fire Superstitions
Watch the campfire and see if you can predict the future...
- If a fire falls into two parts, it hints of a parting to come.
- If a fire won't start, it signals a quarrel is on the way.
- If a spark flies in your direction, you have an enemy.
- If a fire suddenly blazes up, a stranger is nearby.
- If a coal falls at someone's feet, that person will marry soo

Meet Robbie

and Find Out How He Gets Carried Away

Q: How old are you and where do you live?

Robbie: I'm twelve years old and I live in Auburn, Maine.

Q: How did you learn about hot-air ballooning?

Robbie: I'm very lucky because my Uncle Walter has a hot-air balloon. He lets me crew for him and even fly in it!

Q: How do you prepare a hot-air balloon for a flight?

Robbie: You have to get up early for hot-air ballooning because right after sunrise the winds are low, which is ideal for flying. Crewing for a hot-air balloon requires much teamwork. The pilot assigns each crew member a responsibility.

Q: Could you explain how a hot-air balloon works?

Robbie: There are three basic parts of the balloon. The round portion is called the *envelope*. This envelope is 70 feet long and holds 77,000 cubic feet of air! The *basket* is usually made of rattan wicker and is suspended from the envelope by support ropes. The basket carries the pilot and passengers. The best part is the *burner*. The burner's flame creates heat, which converts the cool air in the envelope to hot air. Ballooning is based on this one fact: Hot air rises. The hotter the air molecules get, the more they expand, which creates lift. You heat the air in the balloon to go up, and let the air cool to go down.

Q: What do you like best about ballooning?

Robbie: I love to fly. When I'm flying in a balloon I feel that I'm on top of the world and I can see forever. My dream is that someday I'll get my balloon-pilot's license and have my own hot-air balloon.

Zfact:

The **first nonstop balloon flight around the world** began in Switzerland and ended in North Africa in March 1999. The balloon was piloted by the Swiss Bertrand Piccard and the Briton Brian Jones. In 1932, Bertrand Piccard's grandfather, Auguste Piccard, was the first person to **pilot a balloon into the stratosphere,** which is the layer of the atmosphere that starts about 15 miles above Earth's surface.

Meet Some Kids
Who Are Cleaning Up Their Neighborhoods

These ZOOMers have all been given ZOOMa Cum Laude certificates in recognition of their outstanding contributions to their communities and the environment. We salute them!

ZOOMa Cum Laude

Neil A. of St. Louis, Missouri, nominated **Joshua F.** Joshua thought that there weren't enough places for the animals in St. Louis to live. So he helped **plant over 200** trees, berry bushes, and plants to give food and homes to butterflies, squirrels, and birds.

ZOOMa Cum Laude

Karen L. of Portland, Oregon, nominated **Maria P.** Maria was the grand-prize winner of the "I Love My Park" **billboard contest.** Her design was chosen over 700 other entries, and it was hung all over Portland for an entire year!

ZOOMa Cum Laude

Linda G. of Franklin, Massachusetts, nominated **Timothy and Brian G.** On their mile-long walk to school, Timothy and Brian noticed a lot of trash. So instead of looking at it every day, they decided to **clean it up** and make sure it stayed that way. They hope more kids do the same to keep our environment safe and clean.

When We Pollute

A Poem

Sent in by Hallie B. of Rittman, Ohio.

When we pollute our Earth,
We must not truly see,
What we are really doing
To you and me.
Every little wrapper, every toxic gas,
Every bottle cap, every piece of glass.
We have to work together
To help save our Earth,
So we can really see
What our planet is worth.

ZOA Cum Laude

Phillis M. of Athens, Tennessee, nominated the **Westside School Sixth Grade Victor Team.** The team has volunteered **over 600 hours** at recycling centers, nursing homes, the Humane Society, and Adopt-a-Highway.

ZOA Cum Laude

Sandy R. of Newtonville, Massachusetts, nominated **Mrs. Benjamin's class at the Cabot School.** The kids studied natural habitats at the park near their school and enjoyed it so much that they wanted to do more. So they made a **brochure about the park's history,** constructed a plaque to hang at the park's entrance, and planted wildflowers.

ZOA Cum Laude

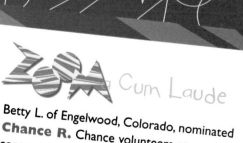

Betty L. of Engelwood, Colorado, nominated **Chance R.** Chance volunteers at a conservatory where he learns how to **rehabilitate injured birds.** Chance even wrote a book about his experiences.

Make Friends with Your Planet

Would you like to **learn** more about wildlife or the environment? Or find out ways you can **help** make a difference? These Web sites contain a wide variety of color photos, articles, facts, games, and more. If you don't have Internet access at home, ask at your school or local library.

National Wildlife Federation
http://www.nwf.org/kids/
Works to protect wildlife. Link to Ranger Rick magazine.

National Geographic Society
http://www.nationalgeographic.com/kids/
Features include articles about science and history. Link to World magazine.

Sierra Student Coalition
http://www.ssc.org
An official branch of the Sierra Club. Includes a student newsletter.

Center for Marine Conservation
http://www.cmc-ocean.org
Marine conservation issues and activities, including an annual coastal clean-up.

National Center for Ecological Analysis and Synthesis
http://www.nceas.ucsb.edu/nceas-web/kids
Ecological information and activities.

Rainforest Alliance
http://www.rainforest-alliance.org
Works to conserve tropical rainforests.

Here are a few things you can do **today** to help save the environment:

- Turn **off** the water while you brush your teeth. You'll save up to 9 gallons of water each time!
- Wash dishes by filling the sink with soapy water instead of leaving the water running. You'll **save** about 25 gallons of water every time.
- Check hoses and faucets for leaks or drips. A dripping faucet or hose can **waste** up to 300 gallons of water each month.

Dress-Up Basketball Relay

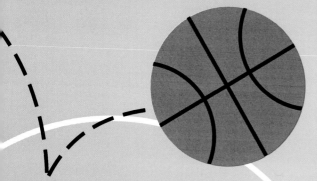

You will need:

- 2 basketballs
- 2 equal piles of oversized or funny clothing

Form 2 teams. Mark off a finish line about 30 or 40 feet away from the starting line. At "Go," 1 player from each team **puts** on all of the clothing in the pile as quickly as possible. Then the player **dribbles** the ball to the line and back. Back at the starting line, the player **removes** the clothes and gives them to the next player to wear. The first team to finish the relay wins.

E-mailed by Ashlee O. of Hollywood, California.

Basketball

A Poem

Sent in by Daniel L. of Succasunna, New Jersey.

When I get the ball I really come
    alive.
I look for a hole, and dribble,
    and drive.
If an unwanted opponent gets in
    my face, a second-hand defender
    puts him in his place.
It's doomsday for the opposing team.
They've got the height, but I've got
    the speed.

Here's a **joke** from Andrea G. of Bolingbrook, Illinois:

Why is basketball such a messy sport?

Answer: Because you dribble on the floor.

Water Balloon Toss

You will need at least 4 players and 1 balloon filled with water for each pair of players.

Pick a partner. Each **pair** should have a water balloon. Teammates should **face** each other and then **line up** next to other pairs to form 2 lines. Players **toss** the balloon back and forth.

Each time the balloon is caught, the players each **take 1 step** backward. The pair who tosses the water balloon **farthest** without breaking it wins.

Bust the Balloon

You will need:

- a few balloons filled with water
- string
- plastic bat or long stick
- blindfold

Tie a string to the end of a water balloon and **hang** it from a tree or pole where there is plenty of room to swing at it. **Blindfold** 1 player and **turn** her around three times. Then **hand** her the bat and **point** her toward the water balloon. Each player takes **3 swings** to try to **bust** the water balloon, as if it were a piñata. If it's a hot day, you might want to **repeat** this game several times.

Ooops

"The most embarrassing thing that has ever happened to me was when I thought my name was called for a trophy at my dance recital, but it was for someone else named Sarah and I was standing there waiting."
— Sarah S. of Quincy, Massachusetts

P.S. You might want to wear a bathing suit for this one!

Warning: Players should be sure to stand clear o the person swinging the b

Don't Spill Relay

You will need **2 paper cups full** of water.

The **winner** of this relay isn't the team that finishes first; it's the team that **spills the least** amount of water.

Form 2 teams. **Give** each team a cup full of water. Make sure they contain **equal** amounts of water.

At **"Go,"** 1 player from each team must **hop** to the finish line while **holding** the cup of water. The next player takes the cup and hops back to the starting line. Once both teams have finished, they should **compare** the water in their cups. The team with the most water left in their cup wins.

Popper Stopper

You will need:
- balloons
- string

Blow up a balloon until it is very full of air. **Knot** the balloon. Then **tie** a piece of string to the balloon and around your ankle.

Try to pop other players' balloons by **stepping** on them. You must **protect** your own balloon. The last player with a full balloon around his or her ankle wins.

Sent in by Stephanie P. of Maize, Kansas.

Make Your Own Chalk

You will need:
- toilet paper tubes
- duct tape
- waxed paper
- throwaway plastic container for mixing
- plastic spoon
- ¾ cup warm water
- ½ cup plaster of paris (You can buy this at any craft store.)
- 2–3 tablespoons of powdered tempera paint

Important Note:
Do NOT pour plaster of paris down your drain. It will harden and clog your pipes! Use only throwaway containers and utensils when mixing plaster of paris.

Completely **cover** one end of a tube with duct tape. **Line** the inside of the tube with waxed paper. **Pour** warm water into the plastic container. Slowly **add** plaster of paris powder in small amounts, **stirring** with the plastic spoon to mix. When the plaster will no longer dissolve, you've added enough.

Stir in the paint and mix well. **Pour** the mixture into the lined tube and **tap** the tube gently to remove air bubbles. Let the chalk dry for a couple of days and then **remove** it from the tube.

Try out your new chalk by creating side-walk murals or playing hopscotch. **See** the next page for a fun sidewalk game called **Fox and Geese.**

P.S. If you would like to make more chalk, just mix up a larger batch. Keep in mind that you usually need three parts water and two parts plaster of paris powder.

Fox and Geese

A Sidewalk Game

Using chalk, **draw** a large circle on an area of pavement. It should be **20–40 feet** across depending on the space available and the number of players. **Draw** 3 or 4 lines across the circle so that it is divided like a **pizza.**

Choose one player to be the **"Fox."** The rest of the players are **"Geese."** The game begins with the Fox standing in the middle of the circle where all the lines meet. The Geese **stand** anywhere on the outside of the circle. At **"Go,"** the Fox tries to tag the Geese. All players must **run** on the lines. If a Goose steps off the lines or is **tagged** by the Fox, that player becomes the new Fox.

P.S. You can also play this by drawing lines in the snow or sand.

Zoinks!

We asked the ZOOM staff to tell us their favorite words spelled with the letter "Z." Here's what they said: Zero, zipadeedoodah, Zimbabwe, paparazzi, zippy, Bozo, Zanzibar, ziti, Zoe, zig and zag, Aztec, Zulu, pizza (who would have guessed?), and gadzooks.

What's yours?

Meet Julio

a Kid Whose Home Really Is on the Range

Q: How old are you and where do you live?

Julio: I'm twelve years old. I live in Rociada, New Mexico.

Q: How did you become a cowboy?

Julio: My grandpa's a cowboy. My dad's a cowboy, and so am I.

Q: What's being a cowboy like?

Julio: It's hard. You have to live on a ranch. There's always something to do every day, like fix fences.

Q: Every cowboy has a trusty horse. Tell us about yours.

Julio: My horse's name is Hector. I've been riding him since I was four years old. Ever since, he's just taken care of me. I've grown up with Hector and he's sort of been my best friend.

Q: What's the best part of being a cowboy?

Julio: My favorite thing to do is to go out and rope cattle. When we catch them we mark them with a brand, a symbol saying they belong to our ranch. I love to rope because I'm with my favorite friend, my horse. It takes a lot of skill to rope, and it just feels good. A donkey is slower than a cow, so I chase the donkey and practice roping his feet. The hardest part about roping is staying on the horse!

Q: Do you like living on a ranch?

Julio: One of the things I like most about living on the ranch is that I get to ride my horse every day. I get to be out here in fresh air. It's a beautiful life up here and I'm not going to move from here for a while.

Want to sound like a cowboy?
Here are a few key phrases to get you started:

Cowboy Talk	Meaning
"That's a real toad floater."	It's raining hard.
"It's time to get into my flea trap."	I'm going to bed.
"I was chewing gravel."	I was thrown by a bucking bronco.

Limbo!

Sent in by Suzy D. of Miamisburg, Ohio.

You will need a **broomstick.** **Music** isn't absolutely essential, but it's highly recommended!

This **African** game tests strength and flexibility. Have one person hold each end of a broomstick. Keep the stick parallel to the ground at all times. The stick should **start** at about shoulder height. After each round, the stick should be **lowered** a few inches. Players take turns leaning back and walking under the stick. Players are out when they **touch** the stick with any part of their body, or when they fall on the floor, or touch the floor with their hands.

How **low** can *you* go?!

P.S. If it's hot outside, try Water Limbo. Use a garden hose instead of a broomstick and wear a bathing suit. **Limbo** under a stream of water. If you get wet, you're out!

Fannee Doolee

likes **drizzle** but not **rain.** Why do you think that is?

Tortilla-flip Relay Race

Form 2 teams. Give a frying pan and tortilla to 1 person on each team. At "Go," the 2 players start **flipping** the tortilla in the pan as they would flip a pancake. While flipping, they **run** or walk as fast as they can to the halfway line, **tag** it, and return to hand off the pan and tortilla to a teammate. If a player **drops** the tortilla, he or she must stop, pick it up, and start flipping again before moving ahead.

E-mailed by Valerie B.

Here's a joke from Carla B. of Cambridge, Massachusetts:

What should a runner eat before a race?

Answer: Ketchup!

44

Ice Cube Melt

You will **need** one ice cube per team. Depending on the size of your group and the temperature outside, you may want to consider **making** extra-large ice cubes by freezing water in paper cups.

Form two teams. Each team should **stand** close together in a circle. The object of the game is to **melt** the ice cube by quickly passing it from one player to the next. Players cannot **drop** it on the ground or put it in their mouths.

The first team to melt their cube **wins!** Or you can **time** the game and **compare** cubes after a certain number of minutes have passed.

Here's a **joke** e-mailed by Jessika. We translated it into Ubbi Dubbi.

Whuby dubo fubish lubive ubin subalt wubatuber?

Ubanswuber: Bubecubause bubebpuber mubakes thubem snubeeze!

You will need:

scissors
garden hose
old rubber glove
rubber bands

Cut the fingertips off an old rubber glove. Fit the wrist part of the glove over the end of the hose and **attach** it tightly with rubber bands. Turn on the hose, **hold** the end of the hose over your head, and watch out for the spray!

Sprinkler Fun

Quarter-Between-the-Knees Relay

Sent in by Suzie F. of Halifax, Nova Scotia, Canada.

You will need **1 quarter per player** and **2 buckets.**

Form 2 teams. Place 2 buckets at the finish line. **Hand** each player a quarter. One player from each team places a quarter between his or her knees and **races** toward the finish line. If the player **drops** the quarter on the way, the player has to **pick it up, return** to the starting line, and start over.

Once the player reaches the finish line with the quarter between his or her knees, the player must drop the quarter in the bucket without using any hands. Then the player **runs** back to the starting line and **tags** the next player. The first team to get all their quarters in the bucket wins.

P.S. If it's a hot day, have a Water Balloon-Between-the-Knees Relay by replacing the quarter with a water balloon. Better make a few extra water balloons in case anyone drops one. You might want to wear a bathing suit!

Fannee Doolee likes **football** but doesn't like **sports.** Why do you think that is?

46

Meet Rachel and Find Out What's Driving Her up a Wall

Q: How old are you and where are you from?

Rachel: I'm twelve years old and I'm from Berkeley, California.

Q: What kinds of things do you climb?

Rachel: I climb anywhere — even in my house. I practice climbing with my coach on a special plastic wall in a gym. But I like climbing outdoors best.

Q: Why did you become interested in climbing?

Rachel: I've never been into soccer, basketball, or volleyball. This sport is really a lot more than just a sport. It's a lot of thinking. It takes so much focus.

Q: Would you like to share any climbing tips?

Rachel: My eyes are always looking everywhere. They're looking up to see what's coming. They're looking down to see where my feet are. I'm sort of short for my age. I have smaller hands that can fit into really tiny holes. Some of the time I can see things on walls that nobody else could even think of using and it really helps me.

Q: Do you ever get scared that you'll fall while you're climbing?

Rachel: No, but I'm always on a rope. It's always safe if you're on a rope.

Q: Why do you like climbing outdoors best?

Rachel: When you climb outdoors there's a lot more air. Then I get to the top and there's a nice view from up there. There's sort of a sense of peacefulness when I'm up there climbing.

'Ulu Maika

'Ulu Maika is a very old Hawaiian game that's a little like bowling. It used to be played with wooden stakes and slices of green breadfruit called 'ulu.

Sent in by Amber of Hoolehua, Hawaii

You will need:

- 2 tennis balls
- 2 two-liter soda bottles
- water
- masking tape or something to mark lines on the playing surface

Fill the bottles with water. **Place** them about 6 inches apart in the middle of the yard or other flat surface. Then **draw** or mark 2 lines extending 30 feet from each of the bottles to create an alley.

Players should take turns trying to **roll** the ball between the 2 bottles, as if they were bowling. The first player who gets the ball between the soda bottles 5 times wins.

P.S. When you and your friends are pros at this, raise the winning score to a higher number to make the games last longer.

Zoops

"The most embarrassing thing that ever happened to me was being chased by a little dog. And a lot of people I knew saw me get chased!"
— Stephen F. of Briarwood, New York

48

Eat Outside

Sent in by Haley F. of Marion, Indiana.

When the weather's nice outside? Grab a blanket a a ZOOMpicnic. Don't fo

Polly's Pocket

You will need:

- 1 banana
- 2 tablespoons peanut butter
- pita bread
- apple slices

Mash the banana in a bowl with the back of a spoon. **Add** peanut butter. **Mix** with an eggbeater or fork. **Cut** the pita in half so you have a pocket. **Spread** the mixture inside the pocket. **Fill** the rest of the pita with apple slices.

Bon Appetit!

My Super Sub
A Poem

Sent in by Trevor W. of Ulysses, Kansas.

Pile on the lettuce.
Pile on the cheese.
Where's the peas?
Ice cream, ham,
even a little Spam.
To make it sweet,
chocolate is a treat.
Top it off with a rubber shoe.
Don't forget the mustard,
ketchup, and pickles, too.
Gee, I'm hungry.
How about you?

Here's a **joke** from Larry C. of Memphis, Tennessee:

What did the doctor say to the banana?

Answer: Are you peeling okay?

Perfect Pasta Salad

You will need:
- pasta (See suggestions below.)
- onions
- celery
- cucumbers
- green peppers
- cherry tomatoes
- Italian salad dressing

E-mailed by Janelle L. of Romeoville, Illinois.

With an adult's help, **cook** the pasta according to the directions on the box. **Drain** and chill. **Chop** the vegetables into bite-size pieces ($\frac{1}{4}$ to $\frac{1}{2}$ cup of each vegetable should be about right). **Mix** with chilled pasta. Add enough dressing to suit your taste. **Refrigerate** until you are ready to head outside for a picnic.

These are our favorite kinds of pasta for making pasta salad:

Farfalle
(far-fah-lay)

Fusilli
(foo-see-lee)

Macaroni
(mack-ah-rone-ee)

Ziti
(zee-tee)

Here's a **joke** from Melanie C. of Tucson, Arizona. We translated it into Ubbi Dubbi:

Whubat hubas fubour lubegs uband flubies?

Ubanswuber: Uba publcnubic tubable.

Irresistible
Ice Cream
Sandwiches

Sent in by Kati H. of Winfield, Missouri

Zfacts:

Next time it's hot outside, make these **tasty** freezer treats and *chill out!*

You will need:

30 cookies (any kind)
ice cream or frozen yogurt (any kind)
optional:
chocolate chips
(or other chocolate for melting)

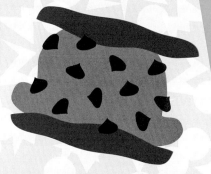

Soften ice cream by letting it sit at room temperature for a few minutes. **Scoop** some ice cream and spread it onto a cookie. **Top** it off with a second cookie and you've made a sandwich!

If you like, you can **roll** the edges of your sandwiches in chocolate chips. Or, you can **dip** your sandwiches in melted chocolate. Melt about a cup of chocolate chips in a microwave-safe bowl for 1 minute. Stir. **(Ask an adult to help you with the microwave.)** Cook 15 more seconds and stir again. Repeat until chips are completely melted. Then dip your sandwiches into the chocolate. Freeze sandwiches until firm. **Enjoy!**

Can't get enough ice cream? If you worked in an ice cream truck, you would have about **5** freezers full of ice cream close by all day. But it's no dream job—on a hot day you might scoop as many as **750** ice cream cones.

According to the *Guinness Book of World Records,* the "most monstrous ice cream sundae ever concocted" weighed **27,102** pounds. Toppings had to be added with the kind of truck used for fixing telephone wires!

Try oatmeal cookies with vanilla ice cream or chocolate chip cookies with strawberry ice cream.

51

Silly Ice

Ask an adult to help you use the blender.

Purple Cow

You will need:
grape juice
vanilla ice cream

Pour grape juice into a tall glass. **Add** ice cream and **slurp** slowly.

Sent in by Joanna C. of Andover, Massachusetts.

"I sure would like to eat one!"

Bodacious Banana Juice

You will need:
blender
1 sliced banana
ice cream
(Strawberry is nice.)
1 cup milk

Put all of the ingredients into a blender and **blend** away. Pour into a tall glass and **enjoy!**

Sent in by Nicole N. of Valparaiso, Indiana.

52

Cream Sodas

Orange Dream Soda

Sent in by Heather and Natalie E. of Loveland, Colorado.

You will need:
blender
1/4 cup orange juice concentrate
2 tablespoons sugar
1/2 cup milk
1/2 cup water
I teaspoon vanilla extract
rolling pin
plastic bag
ice cubes
dish towel

Pour first 5 ingredients (orange juice concentrate through vanilla extract) into a blender. Then put some ice cubes in a plastic bag and wrap a towel around the bag. Use a rolling pin to **crush!** Add the crushed ice to the blender a little at a time and **blend** at high speed. Continue adding ice until the mixture is thick and smooth. Pour into a tall glass and **drink** up!

Z fact:

Borborygmi is the scientific term for the **rumbling in your stomach** when you're hungry. It happens when your stomach walls squeeze together to digest food — only there isn't any food there because you haven't eaten! Instead, the digestive juices and gases splash around and make noise.

Lickable Layered Juice Pops

Sent in by Caitlin B. of Dunn Loring, Virginia, and Will W. of Pella, Idaho.

You will need:
- 3 kinds of juice
- muffin tin
- aluminum foil
- Popsicle sticks

Pour the first kind of juice to **fill** about one-third of each muffin cup. (Don't get carried away — you need to save room for 2 more layers.) Tightly **cover** the entire tin with foil. Using a knife, carefully make a very tiny **slit** in the foil over the center of each muffin cup. The slit should be just big enough for the stick. **Add** a stick to each cup. The foil should allow the stick to stand up straight while the juice freezes.

Chill for 2 hours or until completely frozen. Then carefully **remove** the foil — the sticks should be set. **Fill** each cup another third with a second kind of juice. **Freeze** for another 2 hours. **Pour** in the third layer and freeze another 2 hours.

To get juice pops out of the tin, put the tin in a shallow pan of warm water for 20 or 30 seconds.

Some tasty juice combos to sample:

Citrus: orange and grapefruit juices, and lemonade

Berry Blast: cherry, strawberry, and cranberry juices

Red-White-and-Blue: strawberry and blue raspberry juices, and lemonade

Lemon-Lime: lemonade and limeade

Or make up your own!

Z fact:

Popsicles were originally called **"epsicles"** after their inventor, whose last name was Epperson. He came up with the idea when he saw a glass of frozen lemonade with a spoon in it.

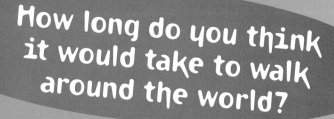

whatZup! How long do you think it would take to walk around the world?

"It would probably take a century or two." — Tashi G. of Seattle, Washington

"I think it would take me ten years to go around the world because I'm small and the world's so big." — Antonio C. of San Diego, California

"I think it would take me a century to walk around the world because I would have to take a lot of stops, and I'm a very slow walker. I would love to sight-see, too." — Alina S. of San Francisco, California

"You can't really walk around the world because most of the world is water and then you'd have to walk on water." — Ryan N. of Sunnyvale, California

"It would take my whole life, beginning to end." — Sean O. of Pasadena, California

What do you think??

Zfact:

The circumference of Earth at its widest point, the equator, measures **24,902** miles.

A Day in the Life of the ZOOMers

5:00 A.M. *Home.* We wake up, take showers, get dressed, eat breakfast, brush teeth, and head out the door for ZOOM.

8:05 A.M. *Makeup and wardrobe.* Since there are seven of us and only one of Sharon, the makeup artist, we take turns getting our makeup done and putting on our ZOOM clothes. When we are done, Jason and Arelitsa, the cast managers, take us to the ZOOMzone.

8:45 A.M. ZOOMzone. This is the place where we hang out when we are not on the set. The ZOOMzone is a big room filled with bean-bag chairs, games, crafts, and other cool things to do during downtime. Since it is our home away from home, we've also brought in some of our

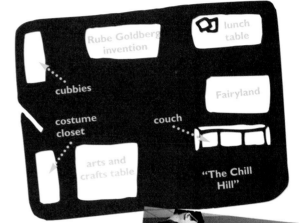

own stuff like posters, games, and stuffed animals. Here, Shea, the drama coach, leads us in a warm-up exercise. We do a different warm-up every day. One exercise we do is all hold hands in a circle and pass a pulse around by squeezing one another's hands.

9:00 A.M. CafeZOOM. We start taping. First up is Claudio, who leaves for the set to do a CafeZOOM segment. He is making Cupcake Cones. While he is on the set, Jenna, one of the associate producers, takes Kenny to another room so that he can learn how to make Kaleidoscopes for a ZOOMdo segment that is being taped the next

day. The rest of us work on this cool project that we started last week. We are building a fairy village out of sticks, leaves, dried flowers, and other stuff that we found outside. Caroline is making a neat-looking fairy swing out of an old tennis ball, some flowers, and some sticks.

9:45 A.M. *ZOOMzinger.* Claudio returns to the ZOOMzone and Jessie, Zoe, and Kenny leave for the set to do a ZOOMzinger. Since these are brainteasers, they have no idea what they are going to do ahead of time so that they don't guess the answer!

10:00 A.M. Chris, the science and math content manager, visits the ZOOMzone to work on an invention with Ray and Alisa. They are trying to build a machine that will put toothpaste on a toothbrush in twenty steps!

10:15 A.M. *ZOOMsci.* Caroline and Jessie head to the set to do a ZOOMsci segment. They are challenged to build a machine that will measure how much air their lungs can hold. While they're on the set, Shea

rehearses an Ubbi Dubbi scene with Ray and Alisa that will be taped later in the week.

11:30 A.M. *Zmail.* Jessie and Zoe are on the set to read a bunch of letters from the ZOOM hamper. It's always fun to see what people write!

12:00 P.M. *Lunchtime.* Everyone returns to the ZOOMzone, where lunch is waiting. Today we're eating Mexican food. We all put on smocks so we don't get food on our outfits. During lunch, Alisa teaches us this cool word game called "Contact."

12:45 P.M. Sharon, the makeup artist, visits us in the ZOOMzone to touch up our makeup and fix our hair.

1:00 P.M. *ZOOMchat.* We go to the set to chat about different topics that have been sent in by viewers. Zoe, Claudio, Jessie, Ray, and Alisa talk about moving. When we're not on camera, we spend time writing in our ZOOMjournals, which we got at the beginning of the season to record our experiences.

1:30 P.M. All of us ZOOMers are back in the ZOOMzone while the crew changes the set. Jason teaches us this really fun circle game called "This Is a Shoe."

1:45 P.M. *ZOOMsci.* Caroline, Kenny, Alisa, and Zoe are challenged to make boats out of Styrofoam trays, balloons, rubber

bands, and washers. Meanwhile, back in the ZOOMzone, Kenny, Ray, and Alisa goof off. They also play a game they invented called "Room-Shot." The object is to get a marble into a cup by rolling it across the room.

2:30 P.M. *Jokes.* We go to the set in pairs to do a bunch of jokes that have been sent in by viewers.

3:00 P.M. *ZOOMgames.* We all change into colorful T-shirts and head to the set to do a bunch of races, including a race where you have to walk with a large ball between your knees and one where you get into a sleeping bag and wriggle like an inchworm!

3:45 P.M. That's a wrap! We all head to wardrobe and change out of our outfits and back into our street clothes. Then we go and clean up the ZOOMzone. (Some days it can really be a mess!)

4:00 P.M. Our day is done! We head home.

Note: This schedule is actually an overview of several days. Typically we tape several segments of one kind in a row, like four CafeZOOMs.

Secret to Ubbi Dubbi
Revealed...

Hey, Jessie.

Just **add** the letters **"ub"** before every **vowel** sound and you, too, can speak Ubbi Dubbi. For instance, if your dog's name is Rover, he becomes Rubovuber. Got it? Grubeat!

Now **go** back and see if you can **read** the Ubbi Dubbi in this book — wube wubouldn't wubant yubou tubo **mubiss** ubout ubon ubanubythubing!

You can also **ubbify** your e-mail or **dubbify** notes to a friend in mere seconds by using the amazing Ubbi Dubbi translator on our Web site at **pbskids.org/zoom**

Yeah, Kenny?

Thubis ubis thube ubend ubof thube bubook. Dubid yubou hubave fubun?

Yubeah. Lubet's gubo buback uboutsubide uband dubo ubit uball ubagubain!

Who is Fannee Doolee?

There is a **pattern** to reading about Fannee Doolee. Fannee Doolee only **likes** things with **double** letters. Here's an example:

Fannee Doolee loves sweets but hates candy.

Notice how there are double letters, **"ee,"** in **"sweets"** but "candy" does **not** have any double letters. Why don't you try to write your own Fannee Doolee and send it to ZOOM!

The Old ZOOMers— Where Are They Now?

What was the best part of being on ZOOM?

Everyone agreed it was meeting great people and hanging out in the ZOOMzone between taping and rehearsing. Jared added that **lunch** was also one of his favorite things!

Last year, you spent the summer taping ZOOM. How did you spend this summer?

"This summer I **danced with a dance group.** We went to Disney for Magic Fun Day, and we danced at Camp Hill, Lauryn Hill's camp. I also work at a dance camp with members of our dance group." — **Lynese**

"This summer I worked at a local repertory theater as an assistant to all the employees." — **Pablo**

"This summer I **went to day camp.** I liked basketball, a game called Newcomb, and swimming. At the beginning of the summer, I went to an intense basketball camp for a week and lost five pounds from running around for five days straight! All the kids called me 'ZOOM.' I also acted in a community theater production." — **David**

"This summer I went on a **trip to Wyoming, Montana, Utah, and Colorado** and went hiking, white-water rafting, kayaking, and rock climbing. Then I baby-sat and went running and swimming with my friends." — **Keiko**

"This summer I was a counselor at day camp." — **Jared**

Alisa and **Zoe** spent the summer doing the same thing they did last summer: working hard and having fun while **taping ZOOM.**

"Being on ZOOM showed me that not only do I want to become **an actor but also a director, a cinematographer, a screenplay writer, and a producer.**" — Pablo

"I want to try to be a professional basketball player, but I think I might try acting and baseball, too." — David

"Now I don't want to be an actor. I want to be a doctor." — Keiko

"I want to be an **actor** even more now." — Jared

"I want to be a **police officer.**" — Lynese

"Since ZOOM, I've realized I want to direct, produce, and **other things besides act.**" — Alisa

"I want to do everything when I grow up, including travel, act, go into the Peace Corps, and help animals." — Zoe

"One of my favorite memories of ZOOM was singing the national anthem at Fenway Park with the other ZOOMers. The ball game was great that day, and I really had fun meeting all the ZOOM fans who came up to say hi to us in the stands." — David

Guess which ZOOMer said this! (Answers are at the bottom of the page.)

1. "I am **seven inches taller** than when I was on ZOOM!"

2. "I finally got my braces off!"

3. "On ZOOM I met **my best and closest friend.**"

4. "I got a sweet **new black kitten.** I named her Jasmine. Sometimes she sits on my shoulder like a parrot."

5. "The CafeZOOMs taught me to be a better cook instead of burning things."

6. "I loved **joking around** on the set with the crew."

7. "I came in **third in the Boston Youth Chess Fest** this year."

8. "I have to admit I **love to shop,** so my favorite places to go with my friends are to the mall and downtown. It's sooo much fun!"

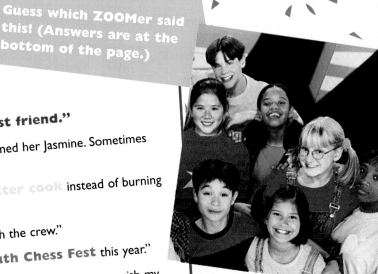

1. Jared; 2. Keiko; 3. Alisa and Zoe; 4. David; 5. Pablo; 6. Alisa; 7. David; 8. Zoe.

What do you like to do outside? What's the coolest game you or your friends ever made up? Have you invented any yummy recipes? E-mail us all about it at pbskids.org/zoom or send it to ZOOM:

ZOOM
Box 350
Boston, Mass.
02134

If you **send** us your ideas,
you will receive a free issue of **ZOOMerang,**
and we might put **your** idea on the show!
All submissions become the **property** of ZOOM
and will be **eligible** for inclusion in all ZOOMmedia.
That means that we can **share**
your **ideas** with other ZOOMers on TV, on the Web,
in print materials, and in other ZOOM ways.

So, **c'mon** and send it to **ZOOM!**